Lookit Cookit

by

Judy Jackson

---
marsons london

First published in Great Britain in 2009 by Marsons

© Judy Jackson 2009

Cover photographs by Daniel Jackson

The author is not responsible for any injury or accident caused by playing the games in this book. Parents are advised to supervise young children using peelers and knives. Special care should be taken when removing trays from the oven and cooking on the hob with boiling liquids or hot oil.

All rights reserved. Without limiting the rights under copyright reserved above, no part of this publication may be reproduced, stored or introduced into a retrieval system, or transmitted, in any form or by any means (electronic, mechanical, photocopying, recording or otherwise), without the prior written permission of both the copyright owner and the publisher of this book.

A CIP catalogue record for this book is available from the British Library ISBN 978-0-9517220-4-6

www.marsonsbooks.com

Printed by Lightning Source

What's in Lookit Cookit?

Contents:

What you *will* find in the book

Games

Experiments

Quiz Questions

Easy Instructions, Called The 'How-To'

Un-Contents:

What you *won't* find in the book

Long Recipes -
Lists Of Ingredients You Don't Have

Things Everyone Knows About -
Like Chocolate Rice Krispies

Bribery -
'Eat Up Your Vegetables, Then You Can Have Dessert'

Cheating -
'Hide The Vegetables In A Sauce'

Let's begin

How to take care in the kitchen

If you're over about 7 you can try these games on your own, but you need to know a few things:

1. Blunt knives are dangerous: they can slip. Use a small sharp knife, hold it firmly and keep the fingers of the other hand out of the way. Please make sure you have your parents' permission to use knives.
2. Boiling water is fearsome. Take care with the kettle. Get help lifting pans and taking food out of an oven.
3. Microwaved food can be very hot. Always lift the cover away from you as steam can burn your fingers.
4. Read through each page. Get everything together before you start the games or cooking. The foods you need are highlighted in colour.

How difficult will it be?

Star rating

* very easy   ** a bit harder   *** for slightly older children

Cooking is about...

Mashing
Squashing
Mixing
Painting
Squeezing
Cutting
Dipping
Pouring

Flavouring
Peeling
Chopping
Melting
Heating
Roasting
Sizzling
Blending

Most of all, it's fun
You're in for some

surprises

Here's a list of
new foods to taste and
the games you can play
while cooking.

List of games

*
(for younger children, with help)

Bouncing eggs
Buzzing and blending
Colouring food
Mixing and mashing
Painting
Rolling and buttering
Shelling
Whisking eggs

**
(may use knives or oven heat)

Baking
Cutting off fish heads
Making pretend wine
Preparing dinner
Rolling and snipping
Rubbing pastry
Squeezing and piping

***
(these also use the hob)

Sizzling
Squeezing and frying

What to make

*

Apple & cabbage salad	9
Banana milk shake	49
Beetroot, cooked	13
Broccoli trees	19
Chocolate digestives	19
Meringues	48
Raspberry yogurt	21
Rolled bread wraps	15
Strawberry soup	73

**

Cabbage, crisp	62
Cheesy feet biscuits	72
Chicken wings, roasted	38
Cup cakes	43
Dates & cream cheese	59
Lemon and ginger tea	52
Pear & watercress salad	53
Roasted vegetables	38
Tomato wine	60

***

Blueberry pancakes	66
Fish, fried	36
Lamb and barley soup	32
Pasta & tomato sauce	54
Potato latkes	68

Colours

*These are fabrics.
Food can also be full of colour and surprises ...*

Coloured water—all natural

Turn over to find out how it's done. Here's a clue: you need one vegetable

Coloured water *

How do you make blue water? Or purple water? It's quick and easy: nothing artificial, all you need is a red cabbage.

The How-to (simple notes to help you follow the pictures)

Take a red cabbage (which is actually purple, but never mind). Cut some slices and put them in a glass of warm water. Then watch: the water will immediately turn a bright, clear blue. After about five minutes the colour will change to a blue purple. By the next day it may change again. Not a drink, but fun.

Crunchy apple and cabbage salad *

Now put some more cabbage slices with some peeled apple in a bowl. You're going to use the microwave to make the apple change colour. Did you know you can actually cook in the microwave? Cover the bowl and cook on full power for about two minutes. Take care when you lift off the cover—the steam that comes out is *hot*. Lift the cover away from you.

The apple will have begun to turn pink from the cooked red cabbage. Now you can make it go red. Spoon over about a tablespoon of olive oil and add a sprinkling of salt and pepper. Mix the cabbage and apple with a fork. The apple will turn red. The salad tastes great. You can eat it warm or cold.

The unexpected ......

What's this? *Pink water?*

Strange things with colours

This is not what you think. The pool in Kew Gardens in London has not been painted pink.

Parts of it were filled with cranberries, more than five million of them, brought from Massachusetts, USA. Here is a box full of cranberries. You made apples turn red, now you can make food turn

pink

Turn over to see how ...

True or false? (answers p74)

1. It takes 200 cranberries to make a pot of cranberry sauce.
2. The juice of the berries is supposed to stop tooth decay.

Painting with food *

Beetroot art

Here's a small piece of beetroot and some plain, thick yogurt. Push the fork into the beetroot.

Then dip it into the yogurt and start to make patterns. It's easy. Of course you can eat it. The beetroot will taste deliciously sweet.

You can buy it ready cooked (but don't buy it packed in vinegar). For a better taste (and more colour) cook it yourself.

Cooking beetroot for painting *

The How-to

You'll need 3 or 4 uncooked beetroot. Cut off the leaves and stalks. Clean the beetroot well with a brush or use a piece of cloth to remove any dirt. Cut them in half and put them in a shallow bowl with about six tablespoons of water. Cover the dish (you can use clingfilm or a plate) and cook in the microwave for about 10 mins. They are done when a knife goes in easily. Take care when you lift off the cover. Steam is very hot. When the beetroot are cool, peel off the skins and you're ready to start painting.

What if … ?

You don't have yogurt?
Use sour cream or crème fraîche, but cottage cheese is lumpy.

True or false? (answers p74)

In America:
1. Beetroot are called beets
2. Biscuits are called cookies
3. Turnips are called eggplant
4. Rice is called white barley

A change from sandwiches *

Sandwiches ...

... can be boring—two bits of bread with something inside.

They taste much nicer if the bread is very thin and there's something crunchy in the filling.

For the next game

you need:

an unsliced loaf of white or brown bread

plain butter, peanut butter or cream cheese

then ... for the crunchy filling, choose any of these:

red or yellow pepper
cooked french beans
carrot, celery, cucumber
stoned dates

Rolled bread wraps *

Take out all the peppers' seeds and white parts. Cut the flesh into strips.

Have ready butter and cream cheese and cool beans (boiled for six mins).

Ask someone to help you cut off the crusts and slice the bread thinly.

Flatten each slice with a rolling pin then spread it with butter.

Put the peppers or the cooked beans at one side of the buttered bread.

Roll them up (but keep them covered otherwise they will get dry and hard).

More ideas

What if ... ?

You like foods with a stronger flavour? Use a different spread like hummus, taramasalata, or pâté. Then you can choose another filling like tinned or cooked asparagus tips. Cream cheese or sweet mascarpone is delicious with olives or dates.

True or false? (answers p74)

In America:

1. Smooth and crunchy peanut butter are made the same way; they add the nutty bits at the end of the process.
2. Hummus is a spread made from ham and mustard.
3. These orange fruits are loquats.

A matter of taste—mild or hot

This is an unusual vegetable. It's called a trombone squash. There's also spaghetti squash which has long thin strings inside. These, and marrows, are mild tasting. So are zucchini or courgettes, which are the same thing but called by a different name. All of them need garlic or spices to bring out the flavour.

These are radishes. They have a bright and powerful taste, naturally hot. A red or green chilli (not in the picture) is a vegetable that needs to be treated with some care. The smallest ones are often the most fierce. Spices that add 'bite' are red paprika, ginger, mustard and pepper.

Cooking in the microwave *

Now you know you can *cook* in a microwave. It's not just for heating.

Before you try these tricks, a few simple rules for the way things cook:

1. It's so much quicker than boiling. Think in seconds and minutes.

2. Exact timing is hard—you can always cook something more, not less.

3. Don't add much water: you need spoonfuls—not cups.

4. To start, cook everything on full power.

5. Take care when you lift the food out—it can be very hot.

The picture above shows some asparagus, cooked for 6 minutes with almost no water.

You may need help using a knife and lifting out hot bowls or plates.

What else can you cook? Here are two easy ideas ...

Cooking in the microwave *

Broccoli Trees

Wash the broccoli and cut four 'trees' starting at the stem end. Put them on a plate with 2 tablespoons of water and a sprinkle of salt. Cook for 2–3 mins. The trees will stay green and crisp. If you want them a bit softer, cook for another minute.

Chocolate Digestives

You need: a fork and a pastry brush (or a clean paintbrush). Break up 12 squares of milk or plain chocolate (about 65g or 2oz). Put them in a shallow bowl and cook for 2–3 mins, till melted. Stir till smooth. Paint the chocolate on to any sweet biscuits. Leave to cool a bit, then make patterns with a fork. Eat when they are cold.

Mixing and mashing *

Most people like yogurt

Most children like fruit yogurt

Most fruit-flavoured yogurts are not made of fruit—they are full of sugar and jam

Why not make your own?

The How-to

You only need 3 things:

500g / 16oz   natural yogurt
2–3 tbsp   sugar
250g / 8oz   fresh raspberries
(8oz is nearly 1/2 pt or 1 cup)

This will make about six pots. You'll never want to eat the jammy ones again.

What if ... ?

You can't find fresh berries?

You can use frozen fruits. Raspberries or blueberries are fine. But frozen strawberries are too wet and don't taste good, so only use the fresh ones. Bananas are easy to find all year round.

Making raspberry yogurt *

Wash the raspberries if they are fresh and drain off the water. Defrost them if they are frozen.

Use a shallow bowl and mash the berries with some of the sugar. Keep pushing and squashing. Then spoon in half the yogurt. Stir it in. Add the rest till you have a thick pink mush. Now taste it. Does it need a bit more sugar? If so add another spoonful. Pour it into pots or cups. Keep them in the fridge till you are ready to eat them. Then ... prepare everyone for a surprise. They taste

delicious

If you're using other fruits, just mash them and then spoon in the plain yogurt.

More about fruit

True or false? (answers p74)

1. Strawberries, which usually grow on the ground, are now cultivated to grow at waist-height making them easier to pick.

2. Lingonberries are grown in Sweden. They are also called cowberries, foxberries or whimberries.

3. Tayberries are eaten on toast in Scotland, for tea or 'tay'.

4. Glass cherries (like these in the picture) were used as currency in the Middle Ages.

Coming up ...   What's inside?

What is this man cutting? It's a whole parmesan cheese. It takes 160 gallons of cow's milk to make this wheel of cheese which weighs 80 pounds. It takes more than a year before it is ready to be cut into about 200 wedges to sell in the shops. It's the perfect cheese for grating on to pasta.

True or false? (answers p74)

In 1969 an Italian man was charged with fraud: he was selling a product he described as 'grated parmesan cheese'. It turned out to be grated umbrella handle.

What's inside a pod? *

Have you ever wondered what's inside a pod?

These are broad beans. Inside the pod is a soft and velvety cushion that protects three or four pale beans. After you cook them it's best to remove the skins as they can be tough. Gently squeeze each one and the bean will pop out.

These are fresh peas. Some pods contain tightly packed large peas—others have small, sweeter ones. Frozen peas are graded for size. They go from the field to the freezer in the space of a few hours, so they keep all their goodness. Fresh peas have a great taste just after they are picked, but lose it within a day or so.

Mysteries inside food

This is an artichoke. It has pointed leaves. These have been cut off to show what's inside. When it's cooked you only eat the bottom part of the leaves. The rest is too hard. Inside is the 'choke'. You must throw away its hairy covering. There, underneath, is the heart. It tastes brilliant.

True or false? (answers p74)
1. Artichokes are part of the thistle family
2. They are eaten with applesauce

What's this?

It's a pumpkin. No, not just an ordinary pumpkin. A vast, humungous

pumpkin

The photos on these pages are misleading. An artichoke is about the same size as a large grapefruit. See how big the pumpkin is by looking at the hands of the boy and his mother scooping out the seeds. It weighed 95 pounds and made enough pumpkin pie and soup for about 80 people.

See what's inside

Do you know what these fruits or vegetables are? Perhaps you recognize the outside, but when you cut them open you may be surprised. The first two pictures are fruits.

Take care handling knives. You should get help with the cutting. Hard objects like these can slip. Hold them firmly and when you've cut them open you will see what's in the middle.

This heavy vegetable is especially tough. It's very hard to cut. Be prepared for a bright surprise when you open it up. The inside looks different from the dull skin.

The last one is a pod. It is the only edible fruit of the orchid family. It starts as a green bean and must stay on the vine for 9 months. Then, it is put out in the sun for many weeks to shrink and develop its flavour and wonderful smell.

The inside story * *

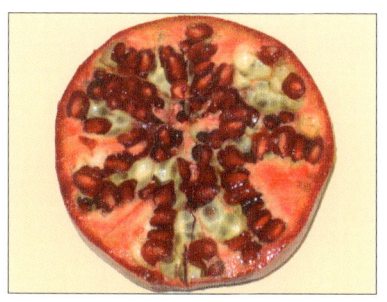

Pomegranate

Cut it in half and count the bright red jewel-like seeds. They are very juicy. Each one has a pip inside it.

Passion fruit

The wrinkly skin shows it is ripe. When you cut it, the first thing that hits you is the amazing smell. Use a spoon to scoop out the inside.

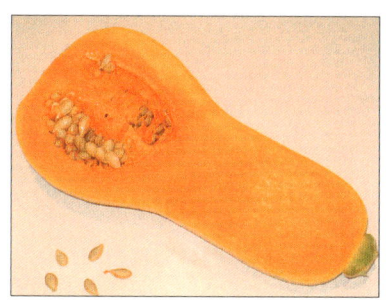

Butternut squash

It is a bright orange colour. If you peel and roast the flesh first, you can turn it into a smooth and creamy soup.

Vanilla pod

Slice through the pod to find tiny black seeds. They look dirty, but scoop them into some sugar. Real vanilla is perfect in ice cream and custard.

More inside stories

True or false? (answers p74)

1. This is the flower of a passion fruit tree.
2. According to Jewish legend a pomegranate has 613 seeds.
3. The old game of squash originally involved two teams who threw bad vegetables across a court.
4. If you cut open a chilli pepper and rub your eyes with your finger, it will be very painful.
5. Most vanilla pods grow in South Africa.
6. Chocolate comes from cocoa beans which are found inside large pods.

Understanding cooking

Cooking is simple: it's about adding or taking away water from food. The heat comes from on top (a grill), from below (a barbecue or hob) or from all round (in an oven). All these methods reduce the amount of water, so to balance this you add a sauce or gravy to make food tasty.

Frying means applying quite a fierce heat from underneath to make food crisp and brown. It's not hard but here are a few things to know which will help you:

1. Food won't cook well in cold or warm oil. Put a little oil in a pan, turn the heat up and count to 40 slowly. Put in a small piece of bread. If it sizzles the oil is hot enough.

2. With fish, meat or pancakes, be careful. Just slide them in. If you throw them in, the oil will splatter and you'll get burned.

3. Turn the food over carefully using long handled spoons.

4. It's a good idea to buy a tube of Aloe Vera Gel and keep it in the kitchen. It's a soothing jelly. If you do get a burn, rub it on immediately and your skin will stop hurting.

So no more warnings — take care and have fun.

Easy, warming, lamb and barley * * *

The How-to

Peel and chop 4 carrots and 3 onions into small pieces. Cut 2 sticks celery into halves. Cut 500g / 1lb boned lamb into cubes and dry them well. Heat 2 tbsp oil in a large pan and fry the vegetables till they go brown. Move them to the side and fry the meat in 3 more tbsp oil. Move the browned meat and vegetables into a deep pot and add 4 tbsp barley. Crumble a beef stock cube with your fingers and add it with 570ml / 1 pt boiling water. Turn up the heat till it bubbles, then turn it down and cook on low heat for 30 mins. Add 280ml / 1/2 pt water and cook for another 45 mins. It will now be a thick stew. To make it into soup, add more water (about 1 cup / 200ml). It tastes delicious and smells wonderful.

Now for something exciting

Are you ready?
Are you brave?

Fish fingers

Yuk or yummy?
Find out for yourself

What's coming now?
Take a deep breath ...

Are you brave enough?

Ask someone to buy you some whole fish with the heads still on. The ones in the picture are sprats. They have tiny bones you won't taste. You can also try this with sardines. Seabass or trout are larger, with a long backbone that you just lift out before you eat them.

Put the fish on a board and find a sharp knife. Cut across the heads.

Yikes, yes, do it!

Then carefully and slowly pull the heads away from the body. What comes out are the guts, the entrails, the insides. When you've had a good look throw them away. Now wash and dry the fish.

Still with me? Get ready...

Frying fish * * *

The How-to

The best place to cook fish is by the sea. If you're on a beach you'll need a barbecue. But it's more likely that you are indoors so you'll want a frying pan instead. Then you need 2–3 tbsp olive oil, a lemon, some black pepper and salt. Start by drying six fish with kitchen paper. Put 1 tbsp oil in the frying pan, heat it gently and after about one minute slide in the sprats, which will sizzle. Cook for 2-3 mins: the bottom will start to go brown. Then, using a flat knife or two long spoons, turn them over, lower the heat and cook again for another few minutes. Small fish cook quicker: fatter ones need more oil and take longer, say 8 mins. Better to undercook a fish rather than leaving it to cook for too long. Lift the fish on to a plate. Add salt and pepper. Cut the lemon and squeeze over some of the juice. Taste it. Surprised? It's very good.

An easier way—buy fish and chips

The best fish should be white and flaky. Only stale fish smells 'fishy'. For the freshest catch you need to be at market early.

True or false? (answers p74)

In Scotland, fish and chip shops sell deep fried Mars bars.

More painting * *

An artist may take a week to paint a picture. Painting food is quick but you have to wait a while to eat the result. Here are two things to try.

Roasted Vegetables

Sticky Chicken Wings

You need peppers, courgettes, parsnips or whatever you like but not peas! Wash and dry them well. Then you need 12 chicken wings (3–4 for each person). Start by making slits with a sharp knife and get together 2 tsp each of oil, soy sauce, dark brown sugar and lemon juice, 4 tsp tomato purée and 1 tsp paprika.

Roasting * *

Cut the vegetables into slices or long strips. Lay them on a sheet of baking paper on an oven tray. Pour some olive oil into a saucer and brush plenty of it over each piece. Sprinkle with salt and pepper. Roast in a hot oven (200C / 400F) for about 30 minutes. Roasted food tastes sweeter than when it's raw.

For the wings mix the oil, soy sauce, brown sugar and lemon juice in a bowl. Stir in the tomato purée and the paprika. Paint this mixture into the slits and all over both sides. Roast on a sheet of paper on a tin at 200C / 400F for 20 mins, then turn them over and cook for another 10–15 mins. Scoop up the bits of sticky sauce and serve with the wings. Yummy!

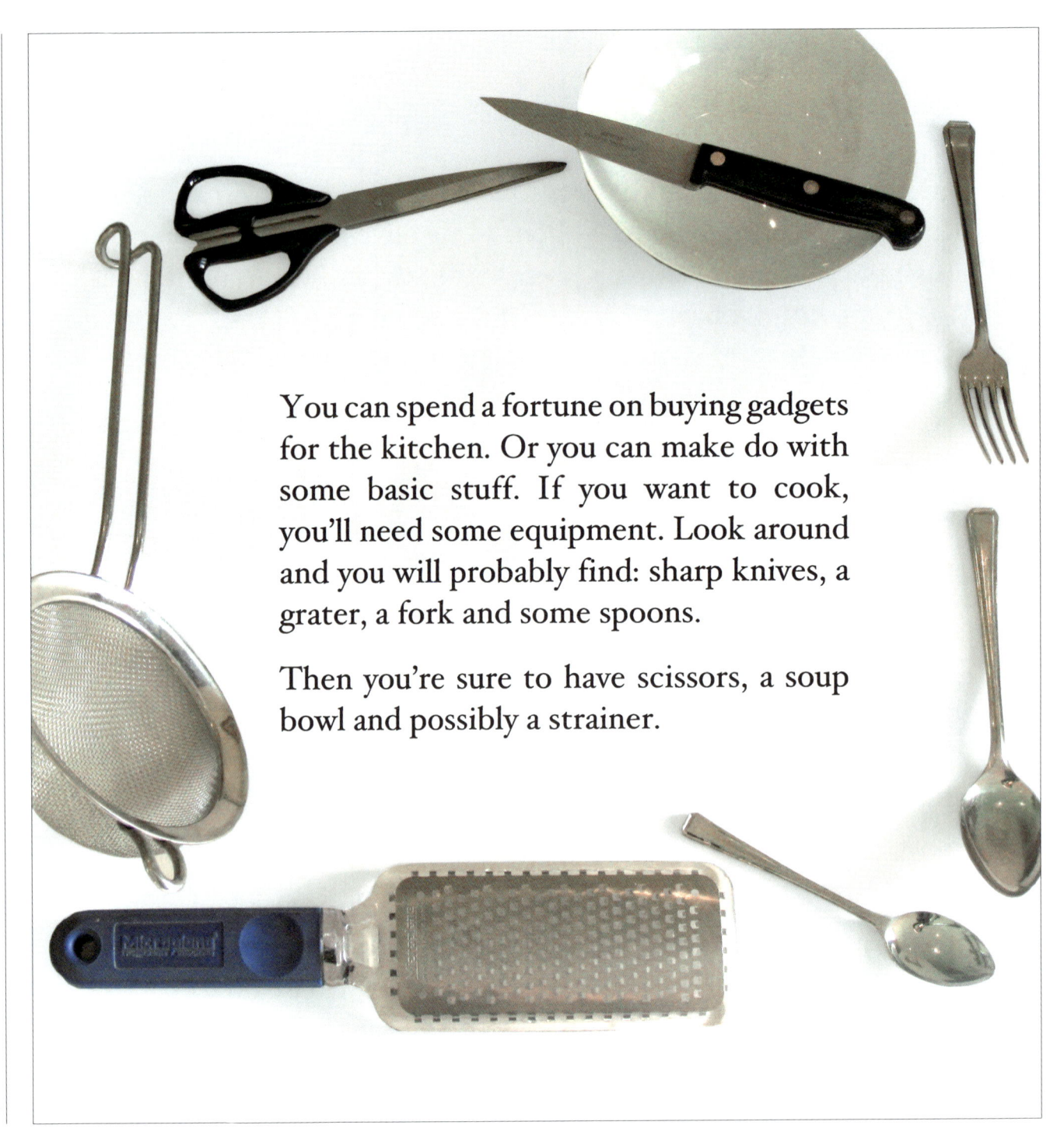

You can spend a fortune on buying gadgets for the kitchen. Or you can make do with some basic stuff. If you want to cook, you'll need some equipment. Look around and you will probably find: sharp knives, a grater, a fork and some spoons.

Then you're sure to have scissors, a soup bowl and possibly a strainer.

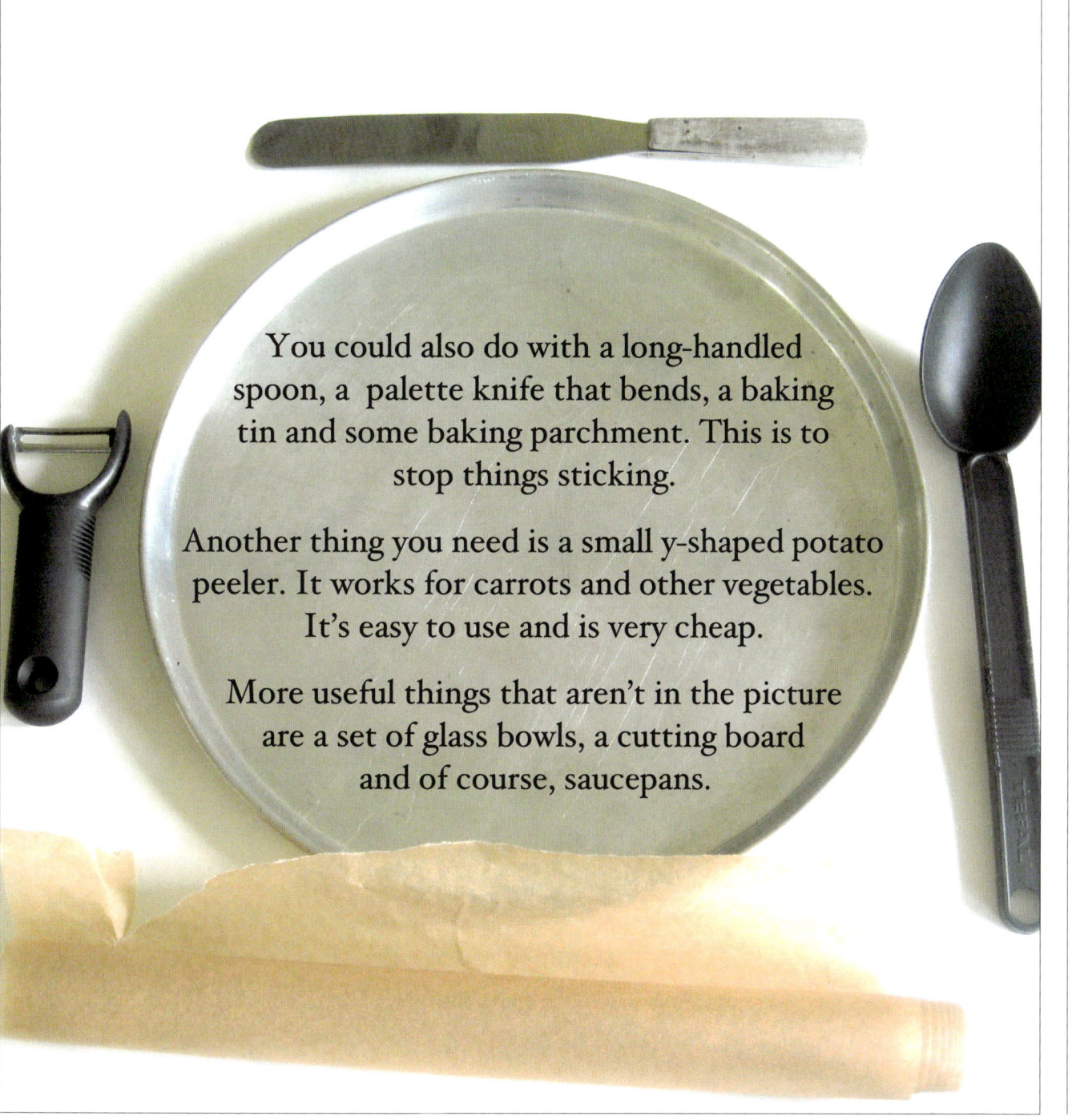

You could also do with a long-handled spoon, a palette knife that bends, a baking tin and some baking parchment. This is to stop things sticking.

Another thing you need is a small y-shaped potato peeler. It works for carrots and other vegetables. It's easy to use and is very cheap.

More useful things that aren't in the picture are a set of glass bowls, a cutting board and of course, saucepans.

Things to know about cakes

Large cakes are tricky to make. It's hard to say how long they'll take to cook—ovens vary. These two have turned out brilliantly but you can end up with an uncooked pudding. Muffins and buns are easier. Small cakes are in fashion and they are now called Cup Cakes. Try them.

True or false? (answers p74)

1. Tiramisu is made with chocolate and lemon. The Italian word means 'mess'.
2. A Dundee cake is a fruit cake with almonds on top.
3. Cheesecake is made with grated cheddar cheese.
4. The icing on a Christmas cake is called Royal Icing.

Cup cakes * *

The How-to

You need a 12-hole muffin tin and some paper cases. Heat the oven to 170C / 325F. In a bowl mix together 115g / 1/2 cup soft butter, 115g / 1/2 cup sugar, 2 large eggs and 1/2 tsp vanilla essence. When this is smooth, stir in 115g / 1 cup self-raising flour. Make sure there are no clumps. Spoon the mixture into the cases. Bake for 15–20 minutes. Leave the cakes to cool.

For the topping, stir a few teaspoons of water into two cups of sifted icing sugar, just enough to make a smooooth mixture. It shouldn't be runny. Spoon this over the cakes. Or mix the sugar with about 3 tbsp unsalted butter and add

colouring

Good things don't last

This is all that's left of some ancient stone pillars in Athens, Greece. Once they were part of a huge temple, now it's just a relic. The remains are still there but the magnificent building has gone.

The gigantic Christmas tree baubles on the next page were outside a New York office for a month. They have gone too.

Food gets made, eaten up and then forgotten. Sometimes things go wrong. Don't get upset. Make something else. All good cooks have had disasters in the kitchen.

45

Some things—like peeling—are best done by hand. But if you enjoy cooking you could do with some help and that means a few machines.

For baking, a weighing machine or cup measure is useful. For mixing, whisking, blitzing, buzzing and blending what you really need are these two wizards, shown on the next page:

an electric food mixer and a blender
(also called a liquidizer)

A food processor (not in the picture) does grating, mincing and slicing, but it's expensive.

47

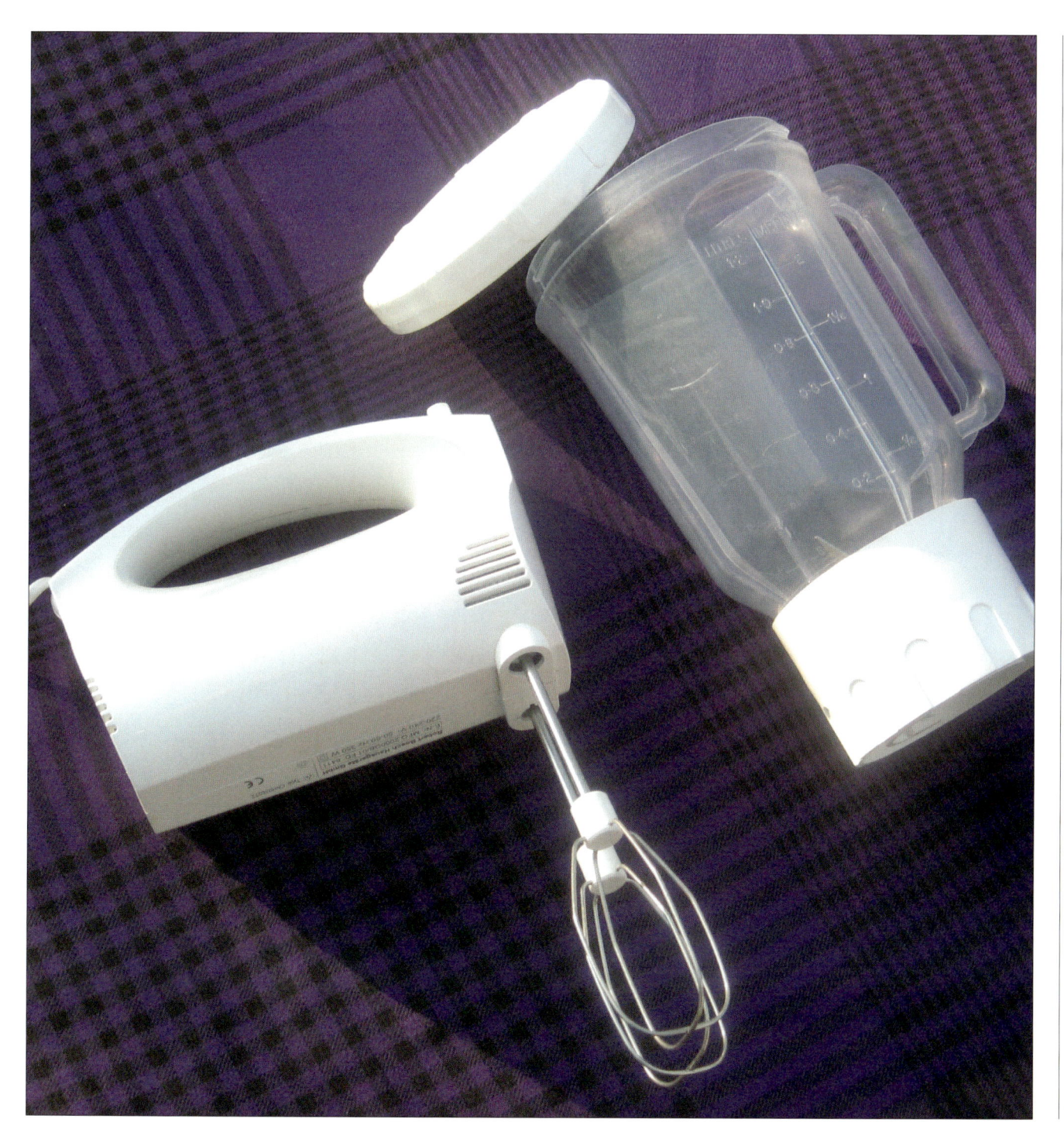

Whisking meringues with the mixer *

The How-to

Take 2 eggs and 100g / 1/2 cup sugar. Separate the eggs (see how p57) and put the whites into a clean dry bowl. Start to whisk. They will begin to get thick. Slowly add a little of the sugar and keep whisking. Carry on till the mixture has doubled in size. It will now be stiff and glossy. Next you need a helper: turn the bowl upside down over her head. If the mixture doesn't fall out it's ready! Cover a baking tin with a large sheet of baking parchment and spoon out rounds of the meringue mixture. If you prefer you can squeeze them out with a forcing bag (see p58). Cook in a low oven 140C / 275F for about an hour. Leave to cool and then slide them off with a palette knife.

Banana milk shake in the blender *

The How-to

Peel three ripe bananas. Put them in the blender with two big glasses of milk. Fix on the top and buzz till smooth. Add 4 ice cubes to make it colder. Or you can freeze bananas (without the peel) and use those and no ice. Add a little sugar if you like and drink it straight away otherwise it goes brown.

True or false? (answers p74)

A phrase used by the French, 'batterie de cuisine', means:

(1) what a chef uses to hit another cook

(2) machines that run on batteries

(3) food that contains butter

Sharing food

Cooking is much more fun if you do it for someone else.

Everybody loves to go out to eat. Even the best chefs enjoy being entertained.

Parents especially are happy to have an evening or weekend meal planned and prepared for them.

Surprise the parents * * *

Tell them that you are going to make dinner and ask if they will do the shopping. Here is the menu (but keep it a secret) and a list of what you need for four people.

The Menu

Pear and watercress salad with blue cheese
Pasta with fresh tomato sauce
Fruit on grape leaves

2 lemons
a piece of fresh ginger
a head of garlic
25 small tomatoes
500g / 1lb pack of pasta
2 ripe pears
1 pack watercress
1 pack mixed salad leaves
olive oil
salt and pepper
150g / 5oz parmesan cheese
180g / 6oz blue cheese

In the winter choose from: grapes, clementines, kiwis, mangos or pineapple

In the summer buy some: nectarines or strawberries, plums, cherries or melon

If you have time you can also make Cup Cakes (see p43 for *The How-to*)

Preparing for the dinner ***

The How-to

The day before:

Make the decorations for the fruit plates. Draw four large leaves on a piece of paper; colour them green and cut them out.

On the day:

Your parents may be tired. Tell them the food will be ready to eat in half an hour. Offer them a soothing cup of Lemon and Ginger tea. You don't need fancy teabags. Peel half an inch of the ginger root, rub it over a grater and put the bits in the bottom of two cups. Squeeze a lemon and add half the juice to each cup. Take care filling the cups with boiling water. Stir in a teaspoon of honey if you like.

The salad starter * *

Now you can get on with cooking the dinner.

First make the salad. Get everything together. Tip the washed leaves into a bowl. Peel the pears and cut them into slices. Put them on a plate. Cut a lemon in half and squeeze the juice into a glass. Pour half the juice over the pears. This is to stop them going brown. Break off a few pieces of the blue cheese and arrange on the leaves with the pears.

Spoon about 3 tablespoons of olive oil into the glass with the rest of the lemon juice. Stir in a little salt and pepper and *just before you serve it*, drizzle this over the salad.

For the pasta, grate plenty of parmesan cheese into a bowl.

The main course * * *

10-minute tomato sauce for pasta

Cut the washed tomatoes in half. Pour about 3 tbsp olive oil into a large frying pan, turn on the heat and wait for a minute. Put the cut tomatoes in the pan. Cook on a high heat for about five minutes, mashing them slightly with a long-handled spoon, as they fry. Take care— they sizzle. While they are cooking break off 3 cloves of garlic. Take off the papery skin and crush them (use a garlic crusher or rub them over a grater). Stir the garlic in with the tomatoes, sprinkle over salt, black pepper, a teaspoon of sugar and a cup of water. Turn the heat down a little and after another five minutes the cut tomatoes will have turned into sauce. Turn off the heat. Boil a large saucepan of water, add a teaspoon of salt and the pasta. Cook for the time it says on the packet (usually about ten minutes). Then drain the pasta through a colander and divide it into four bowls. Spoon over the sauce and serve with cheese and butter.

The fruit plates * * *

These are the winter fruits. Cut the pineapple down into four and cut the flesh away from the skin. Slice it and arrange as above. Peel and slice the kiwis. Cut the mangos down into two chunks either side of the stone part in the middle. Cut lines across to form cubes and push up from underneath. Cover the whole dish with clingfilm. When you're ready to serve the fruit put it on plates with the paper leaves. Relax. Enjoy the end of your brilliant meal.

Afterthoughts

What if … ?

You don't fancy the blue or parmesan cheese? Use brie in the salad and grated cheddar on the pasta.

You don't want to make painted leaves? Look for fresh ones in a garden or park (see the picture of figs above).

The washing up

Someone has to do it—and it shouldn't be the guests (or in this case the parents).

While you clear up—leaving the kitchen spotless to the last shiny tap—think about life working in a restaurant:

1. Imagine washing up every day. It's a poorly paid job. Being at school is much more fun.

2. A sous-chef (French for 'undercook') spends all day doing repetitive tasks, like chopping vegetables.

3. Waiters never eat meals at normal times. Staff are fed before or after customers.

Can you make an egg bounce? *

It sounds impossible. Egg shells are brittle and they break easily. Here's a game. See what happens if you drop a raw egg. If it falls on to any hard surface—even from a height of a few inches—it will crack.

But—put a thick towel on the floor, cover it with a sheet of clingfilm and then drop the egg. First hold the egg six inches above the towel, then drop it. Then hold it higher. It won't break. It will

bounce.

To separate an egg

Break the shell open and tip the egg into a cup. Hold a clean hand over a bowl, open your fingers slightly and pour the egg from the cup into your palm. The white slips through your fingers into the bowl but the yolk stays in your hand.

Squeezing * *

When you think about squeezing what do you imagine? Toothpaste? Making juice from oranges or lemons? There's a lot more ... and all you need is a piping or forcing bag. The professional ones come with 'nozzles'—metal or plastic pieces that fit at the end of the bag—and force the food into different shapes.

What can you squeeze, or pipe? Anything without lumps like sugar icing or meringue mixture. Perhaps try whipped cream.

The How-to

The secret of success with a piping bag is never to fill it too full, otherwise when you squeeze, it squirts everywhere. If you have a piping kit, screw on the nozzle you want (small hole is the best) and fill the container with icing. Put on the top and gently squeeze out the icing—on to a cake or biscuits. You can practise by trying to write your name on a plate. With cream you need a piping bag with a larger nozzle. Spoon in the whipped cream and squeeze it on to cakes, meringues, bananas or berries.

Piping * *

To pipe rosettes, squeeze gently from above, making a circle, then lift up the bag and give it a slight twist before going on to the next one.

What if ... ?

You don't have a piping bag?

Make your own with a plastic bag. Cut 1 cm off one of the bottom corners to make a hole. Then spoon in a little cream. Fold over the top and then squeeze.

You don't have icing or cream?

Use a pack of cream cheese. Squeeze it through the nozzle (it's harder with the plastic bag) and force it on to bread, crackers or stoned dates.

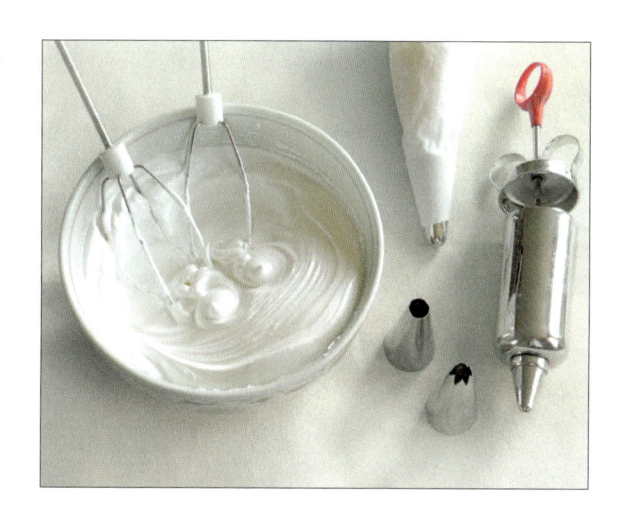

Tomato juice that looks like wine * *

For this game you need a little patience. Try this in summer when tomatoes are cheap and tasty. You will need: two bowls, a strainer, a large clean handkerchief and a jug. The 'wine' is made from 1kg / 2lbs unpeeled tomatoes, 1 tsp salt, 1 tsp sugar, 6 basil leaves and a little ground black pepper.

Cut the tomatoes roughly and put everything into a food processor. Buzz it up till you have a thick tomato mush. Put the strainer over the bowl, put the handkerchief on top and carefully pour some of the mixture in. *Don't press it* and stop when the lined strainer is full. Tie the handkerchief loosely on top and put the bowl and the rest of the mixture in the fridge. Now all you need to do is wait (it takes several hours).

An extraordinary drink * *

A clear liquid will appear at the bottom of the bowl. After about an hour pour this into a jug and add more of the tomato mush to the strainer. Remember *don't stir or push it down* or it will go cloudy (see below). When you have added all the mush, and the juice has dripped through, pour the clear tomato-flavoured essence into glasses. It's great!

True or false? (answers p74)
1. A love apple is an old-fashioned name for a tomato
2. Muscovado sugar comes from Moscow

More playing with the microwave * *

Crisp and tasty cabbage

(Please ... don't moan, try it.)

Everyone knows that fruit and green things are good for you. But when you boil them in a pan of water you lose the vitamins. Fruit and vegetables cooked in the microwave need little or no water.

The How-to

Wash 6 large cabbage leaves, roll them up and then cut the roll into thin slices with a sharp knife. Shake out the cabbage into a shallow bowl or soup plate and cover with another plate. Cook for two minutes. Take care when you lift off the plate—steam will come out, so lift it away from you. To make it tastier add salt or a few drops of soy sauce.

A dessert in 10 minutes * *

Quick apple puddings

The How-to

You need: 2 green apples, 2–3 tsp sugar, 2 or 3 crushed meringues and a cup of thick cream or yogurt.

Peel the apples and cut them into pieces without the core. Put these on a large plate and sprinkle over two dessert spoons of sugar. Cover and microwave for about four minutes. Mash the apple with a fork. Leave it to cool. Find two wide glasses and put some of the crushed meringue in each one. (If you don't have any meringue you can use crushed biscuits or a slice of plain cake.) Then put a layer of the apple in and top it with a layer of cream or yogurt. If you prefer use custard (on the right in the picture) but it will be sweeter. Or just make …

Baked Apple

Easy as 1, 2 3. You need an apple corer to take the centre out of 1 large cooking apple. Push 2 tsp brown sugar in the hole, add 2 tsp water and microwave for 3 minutes.

Time for tea

This is the window of a pastry shop in Hungary. Elegant cakes like these are found in many countries in Europe. They're not easy to bake. But smaller things are simple to make at home.

What a strange teapot

It's very old and the spout is in the shape of a camel's head. Tea can be made from herbs like mint and camomile but rosemary or chive tea? No thanks.

Blueberry pancakes * * *

The How-to

You need a frying pan or griddle, a palette knife and

1 cup	plain flour
2 flat tsp	baking powder
1 large	egg
1 tbsp	plain or vanilla sugar
1 cup	milk
1 cup	blueberries
6–8 tbsp	sunflower oil
To serve:	butter, maple syrup

Wash and drain the berries and dry them with paper towels. Sift the flour and baking powder into a bowl, add the egg, sugar and a little milk and stir to mix them all together. Beat well to get rid of any lumps and then stir in the remaining milk. If you like, get help with the frying.

Put a little oil in a frying pan or griddle and when it is hot spoon some of the batter into small heaps, not too close together. The mixture starts to set immediately. Sprinkle on a few blueberries and watch while small bubbles appear on the surface. Flip over the pancakes with a palette knife and cook the other side for about a minute.

Blueberry pancakes * * *

Put the cooked pancakes on a sheet of baking parchment on a tray and keep them warm in a very low oven 130C / 250F. Keep going till you've used up all the batter. To serve them, pour over a little maple syrup.

What if ... ?

You don't have any berries? Plain pancakes are good, even cold with butter.

There's no maple syrup? Just use golden syrup.

True or false? (answers p74)
1. The world's biggest pancake was 15 metres in diameter and weighed 3 tons
2. Blueberry juice is used as ink in royal palaces

Crispy potato pancakes (latkes) * * *

The best part of making these is squeezing the potatoes. They are full of a starchy liquid which you squeeze out. If you leave the mixture to stand it will go brown. You need: 4 medium/large potatoes, 1 onion, 2 small eggs, 2 tbsp matzo meal (from a Jewish deli), salt, pepper and oil for frying. To go with them: sausages, or sour cream and apple sauce.

The How-to

Start by grating the peeled potatoes and onion. Use a hand grater or the grating disc of a food processor. Squeeze the grated vegetables in your hands letting the chalky white liquid drip into a bowl. Before you throw it away, see how it turns into a thick starch.

Making the potato latkes * * *

Beat the eggs in a large bowl and stir in the potatoes and the matzo meal. Then add a few grinds of black pepper and plenty of salt—more than a pinch and less than a teaspoon. Taste the mixture even though it's raw: too little salt will make it bland. Add the salt gradually, tasting as you go. Pour 1/2 inch of oil into a frying pan and heat it for about a minute.

Place spoonfuls of the mixture all over the pan, not too close together. The oil should sizzle as soon as the first pancake goes in. Flatten them with a long spoon so they are about 1/2 inch thick and fry until the underside is crisp and brown. Turn them over with a bendy palette knife and brown the other sides. Drain on paper towels and serve immediately.

Table decorations

What do you need to make a table look pretty? Not expensive flowers. This one just has a covering of snow, but you can't eat off it. When your parents ask you to set the table, you can add something unusual. If you go for a walk you might find some leaves or pine cones. Or ask if you can use candles or tea lights.

Make your own

This is a table for a doll's house. If you like playing with polymer clay (Fimo or Sculpy) you can make models like these as table decorations. This collection of beef, sausages, lemons, chocolate, tomatoes and cheese took longer to produce than a proper meal. The tiny copies of real food (see the size from the leaves in front) were baked in an oven till they hardened.

Using your hands—Cheesy biscuits * *

Remember playing with sand and rolling it through your fingers? Pastry is made by rubbing fat into flour, then adding liquid. These biscuits are even easier.

The How-to

100g / 1 cup	grated cheese
50g / 1/2 cup	plain flour
1/4 tsp	baking powder
25g / 2 tbsp	soft butter

Put all this into a bowl and rub it between your thumb and fingers (clean hands, please). Keep going till you can squeeze it into a ball. Put the cheese pastry on to a board lightly sprinkled with flour. Cover with a sheet of clingfilm (to stop it sticking) and roll it out with a rolling pin. Cut it into shapes and lift them with a palette knife on to an oven tray covered with baking paper. Use up all the pastry, making new balls and rolling them out again. Put the tray in the fridge while you heat the oven to 190C / 375F. Cook the biscuits for 10 mins till they are brown. They will be a bit soft, but harden as they cool. Animal, hand or foot shapes may look better but plain rounds taste as good.

Buzzing or blitzing—Strawberry soup *

Hungarian cold cherry soup is famous. This strawberry soup is made by buzzing up ripe red berries with some sugar. You can eat it anytime you like. If you have it at the end of a meal you might want to add some vanilla ice cream and a leaf of mint to make it special.

The How-to

Use an electric blender. Buzz 500g / 2 1/2 cups strawberries with 2 tbsp sugar till it looks quite smooth. Taste it and, if you want to, add one or two extra spoonfuls of sugar. In the winter strawberries have far less flavour and sweetness. Next stir in some iced water (5 to 10 tbsp) to thin it down and make it cooler. Scoop a ball of ice cream into each bowl.

True or false?

The answers

Page 11 – 1,2 both true

Page 13 – 1,2 true, 3,4 false

Page 16 – 1 true, 2,3 false

Page 22 – 1,2 true, 3,4 false

Page 24 – true

Page 26 – 1 true, 2 false

Page 30 – 1,2,4,6 true, 3,5 false

Page 37 – true

Page 42 – 1,3 false, 2,4 true

Page 49 – 1,2,3 false

Page 61 – 1 true, 2 false

Page 67 – 1 true, 2 false

How did you do?

How many did you get right?

    10-20 good

    21-30 excellent

    30-34 brilliant

Want to know more?

You probably know these are olives. Maybe you didn't know:

Aubergines are called eggplants in America.

Hummus is made from chickpeas.

Small orange fruits are kumquats. Loquats are big and paler.

Tayberries are not eaten on toast and tay doesn't mean tea.

Artichokes are eaten with mayonnaise, butter or vinaigrette.

The best vanilla comes from Madagascar.

Tiramisu and cheesecake are both made with creamy cheese.

Batterie de cuisine means cooking equipment.

Muscovado sugar comes from Mauritius or the Philippines.

76

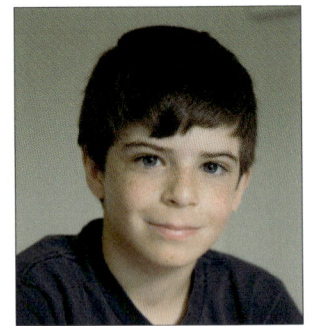

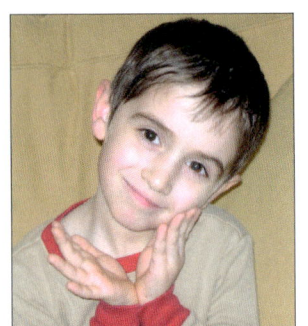

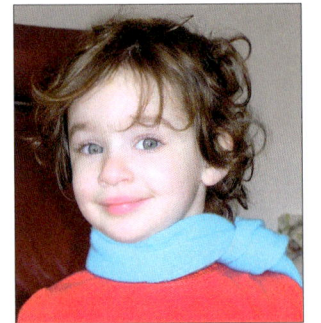

Dedication

This book is for children everywhere, but is especially for my grandchildren. Many of them are brilliant cooks. Others are still at the playing stage. The idea for Lookit Cookit came from happy hours spent eating, playing and cooking together in my kitchen. So thank you

Rachel

Noah

Rebecca

Sam

Akiva

Amos

Alice

Shoshana

Yannai

Aderet

Micah

Other books by the same author

Judy Jackson has writen nine previous books

Food :
: The Home Book of Jewish Cookery
Microwave Vegetable Cooking
A Feast in Fifteen Stories
The Jewish Kitchen
The Passover Menu Planner
The Essential Jewish Cookbook

Memoir:
: Tess Blackburn

Fiction :
: The Camel Trail
(winner of World Gourmand Award for best Food Literature Book published in UK in 2007)
Trio (to be published shortly)

Restaurant reviews:
: 'Time Out—Eating Out in London'

© Copyright 2009—Judy Jackson

No part of this publication may be reproduced without prior written permission of the author.

The author is not responsible for any injury or accident caused by playing these games. Parents are advised to supervise young children using peelers and knives. Special care should be taken when removing trays from the oven and cooking on the hob with boiling liquids or hot oil.

www.lookitcookit.com

LaVergne, TN USA
31 January 2010
1684LVUK00002B